DATE DUE

OC 24 '80			
OC 31 '80			
NO 21 '83			
4			
Lay			
AP 4 '86			
JAN 1 2 1987			
FEB 2 3 1987			
NOV 2 1987			
DEC 1 4 1987			
MAY 9 1988			
MAR 7 1991			

DEMCO 38-297

THE SUPER DUPER AMERICAN HISTORY FUN BOOK

THE SUPER DUPER HISTORY FUN BOOK

BY
Karen Markoe & Louis Phillips

Graphics by Nicholas Krenitsky
Drawings by Tom Huffman

Franklin Watts / New York / London / 1978

Photographs courtesy of: N.A.S.A.: p. 10; Library of Congress: pp. 11, 36 (1), 37 (6), 60, 84 (bottom left); Museum of the City of New York: p. 12; Harry S Truman Library: p. 13; New York Public Library Picture Collection: pp. 14, 16, 19, 32, 35, 47, 72, 84 (top right); European Picture Service: p. 17; F.W.I.: pp. 26, 28, 37 (8, 10); Franklin D. Roosevelt Library: pp. 27, 71; Rhode Island Historical Society: p. 29; American Foundation for the Blind: p. 37 (4); The White House: p. 37 (9); United Press International: pp. 36 (3, 7), 64; Wide World Photos: p. 36 (5); Association of American Railroads: p. 48; National Archives: pp. 61, (Navy Department) 63; United Nations: pp. 37 (2), 67 (top left); Virginia Department of Conservation: p. 67 (bottom); Rushmore Photo, Inc.: p. 70; National Museum of History and Technology, Smithsonian Institute: p. 75; N.Y. Convention and Visitors Bureau: p. 78; YIVO Institute for Jewish Research: p. 84 (center); Patti Cappalli for Jerry Silverman Sport: p. 84 (bottom right).

Library of Congress Cataloging in Publication Data

Markoe, Karen.
   The super duper American history fun book.

   SUMMARY: An activity book of word games, puzzles, and quizzes using names, places, and dates from American history.

   1. United States—History—Miscellanea—Juvenile literature. [1. United States—History—Miscellanea] I. Phillips, Louis, joint author. II. Krenitsky, Nicholas. III. Title.
E178.3.P55   973   77–15530
ISBN 0–531–01468–1

CONTENTS

To
Bobby
Ricky
Lauren
&
Nancy
... with love

Author's note

The purpose of this book is to encourage you, the reader, to have fun with the names, places, dates, and objects associated with American history. By playing with the material presented, by solving the puzzles, by guessing the answers, we hope that your interest in American history will grow and that you will go on to other books to learn more about the people, places, and things presented.

Karen Markoe
and
Louis Phillips

BECOME A

HISTORICAL DETECTIVE

CAN YOU SEP A RATE

Some of the people on the list are real people in American history. Some are made up, or fictional, characters. Which are real and which are fictional? Be careful now. Some names are tricky.

1. Paul Revere
2. Wyatt Earp
3. Huckleberry Finn
4. Casey Jones
5. Lizzie Borden
6. Jesse James
7. Pocahontas
8. Popeye
9. Clark Kent
10. Calamity Jane

FACT FROM FICTION?

ANSWERS

Real People

1. Paul Revere was the revolutionary patriot who rode from Charleston, Massachusetts, to Lexington, Massachusetts, on April 18, 1775, to warn the colonists that British troops were approaching.

   What most people don't know is that along the way, British soldiers captured him and took his horse. They soon released him, and promised to return his horse, but never did.

2. Wyatt Earp, gambler and sometime lawman of Tombstone, Arizona, was involved in the gunfight at the O.K. Corral in 1881. He is often portrayed, probably wrongly, as one of the great heroes of the Wild West.

4. Casey Jones, the railroad engineer in the ballad that bears his name, rode the "Cannonball Express." Born near Cayce, Kentucky, he was always known as "Casey." His real name was John Luther Jones.

5. Lizzie Borden was accused of murdering her father and stepmother, in 1892. Though she was found innocent by the court, most of her neighbors were still convinced that she had committed the crimes. A popular rhyme tells the story:

   Lizzie Borden took an axe
   And gave her mother forty whacks,
   And when she saw what she had done,
   She gave her father forty-one.

6. Jesse James led a life of crime until he was shot to death in 1882 by Robert Ford, a member of his own gang who killed James to get the large reward offered by the U.S. government.

7. Pocahontas was the Indian princess given credit for saving the life of John Smith in Jamestown, Virginia, by appealing to her father, Powhatan. Later, Smith and Pocahontas were married. In his diary, Captain Smith called Pocahontas "the king's dearest daughter."

10. Calamity Jane, a friend of "Wild Bill" Hickok, could shoot and ride as well as any frontiersman. Her real name was Martha Jane Burke.

Fictional Characters

3. Huckleberry Finn, the boy who floated down the Mississippi River on a raft, was created by the author Mark Twain.

8. Popeye is the cartoon sailor with the big muscles who gulps down cans of spinach for extra strength.

9. Clark Kent is the newspaper reporter who changes himself into Superman.

THE CENTURY GAME

A century is a hundred years. We are living in the twentieth century. It began on January 1, 1901, and will end on December 31, 2000. These are the dates of the five centuries that came before ours:

Fifteenth century	1401–1500
Sixteenth century	1501–1600
Seventeenth century	1601–1700
Eighteenth century	1701–1800
Nineteenth century	1801–1900

Do you know in which century . . .

. . . the first person walked on the moon?

ANSWER:

The twentieth century (1969).

. . . Columbus discovered America?

ANSWER:

The fifteenth century (1492).

. . . the Civil War was fought?

ANSWER:

The nineteenth century (1861–1865).

LooKING SHARP

Here is a photograph of Hester Street, in New York City.
How do you know the photograph was not taken recently?
In what year do you think the photograph was made?

12

HARRY S TRUMAN

When President Franklin D. Roosevelt died in April 1945, Harry S Truman became President. World War II was just ending, and the new President helped the nations of Europe to recover from the war.

Truman believed the government should help all the people. In the election campaign of 1948, he announced his plan for carrying out that belief, a program he called the Fair Deal. In that year he was elected to a four-year term of his own.

At first glance, some of these pictures of Harry Truman seem to be alike. But look again. Only two are actually identical. Can you find them?

Pictures 4 and 6 are identical.

THE FIRST?

1. Harvard was the first ———?

2. George Washington was the first ———?

3. Jamestown was the first ———?

4. Jackie Robinson was the first ———?

5. Elizabeth Blackwell was the first ———?

6. The Pilgrims and the Indians celebrated the first ——— together?

7. The freedoms of speech, press, religion, and assembly are guaranteed in the First ———?

8. Lexington and Concord was the first ———?

Can you guess in which century these events occurred?

THIS IS GOING TO BE A TURKEY!

CAN YOU GUESS?

You are not supposed to know the answers to these questions. The object of the quiz is to see how well you can guess. Just make the best guess you can.

1. In 1790, the population of the United States was (*a*) 3,929,214; (*b*) 5,987,187; (*c*) 10,456,198; (*d*) 34,987,654.

2. In 1790, the population of New York City was (*a*) 10,000; (*b*) 25,000; (*c*) 50,000; (*d*) 200,000; (*e*) 1,000,000.

3. In 1861, the number of slaves in the South was: (*a*) 1,000; (*b*) 10,000; (*c*) 1,000,000; (*d*) 2,500,000 (*e*) 3,500,000.

4. In 1880, the population of the United States was (*a*) 2,000,000; (*b*) 10,000,000; (*c*) 50,000,000; (*d*) 80,000,000.

5. In 1900, the average yearly salary of a teacher in the public school system was (*a*) $325; (*b*) $650 (*c*) $900; (*d*) $1,200.

6. In 1973, the number of passenger cars manufactured in the United States was (*a*) 5,213,786; (*b*) 9,667,152; (*c*) 17,567,784; (*d*) 35,089,186.

7. As of January 1, 1977, the population of the United States was approximately (*a*) 78,000,000; (*b*) 109,214,000; (*c*) 167,987,000; (*d*) 215,115,000; (*e*) 398,987,000.

ANSWERS

1. (a)
2. (c)
3. (e)
4. (c)
5. (a)
6. (b)
7. (d)

DO YOU RECOGNIZE THIS?

1. The object pictured here is (*a*) a sled; (*b*) a pillow; (*c*) a pistol; (*d*) a pill box; (*e*) a pillory.

2. It was used by (*a*) the Puritans; (*b*) the plains Indians; (*c*) Civil War soldiers; (*d*) the Eskimos; (*e*) manufacturers of automobiles.

3. The object was used as (*a*) a place to store food; (*b*) a signpost for a tavern; (*c*) a means of punishing people; (*d*) a mold for making candles; (*e*) a place to put mail.

Study the photograph carefully. How do you know it was not taken recently?

LooK SHARP

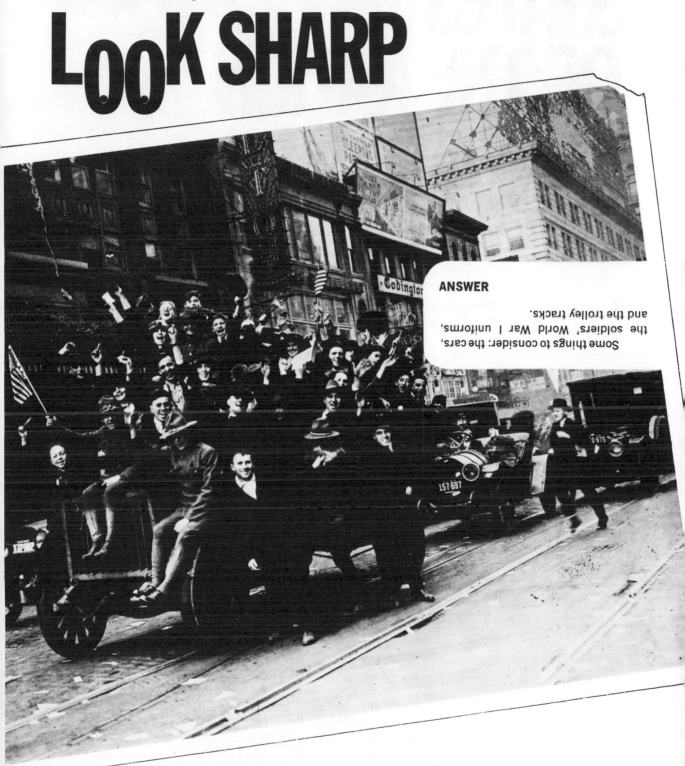

ANSWER

Some things to consider: the cars, the soldiers' World War I uniforms, and the trolley tracks.

STATES OF THE NATION

Can you identify the following States of the United States?

1. The name of this state means "green mountain" in French.

2. The Mormons wanted to name this state Deseret, but Congress chose another name.

3. This state was the first state to grant women the right to vote.

4. This state is called "the Volunteer State," because so many of its male citizens volunteered to take part in the war with Mexico.

In the following block of letters, the names of ten famous native American tribes can be found by reading the letters from the bottom up, from the top down, or across from left to right or right to left. Can you find all ten tribes? *Hint:* Use tracing paper.

INDIAN SEARCH

```
S H K E N P L O I P P
A S I O U X A N R U U
W C O M M A N C H E E
O S W C R E E K Y B L
I E A P A C H E L L O
K O M O H A V A N O N
K I O S E M I N P F I
N O T T A W A C R E M
A L G O N Q U I A N E
A L G O N P U E B L S
```

The tribes to look for are the Kiowa, Apache, Comanche, Sioux, Seminole, Navaho, Algonquian, Ottawa, Pueblo, and Creek.

SOLUTION

```
S L B E U P N O G L A
E N A I U Q N O G L A
M E R C A W A T T O N
I F P N I M E S O I K
N O N A V A H O M O K
O L L E H C A P A E I
L B Y K E E R C W S O
E E H C N A M M O C W
U U R N A X U O I S A
P P I O L P N E K H S
```

PICTURE PUZZLE

The pictures below provide clues to the names of famous
Americans. Can you put the picture clues together so that
they form the name of the person asked for?

EXAMPLE:

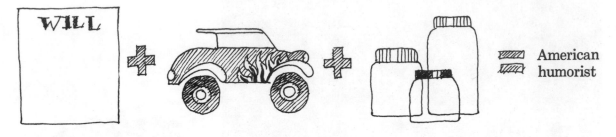

ANSWER:

(sɹɐɾ + poɹ + llᴉʍ) sɹǝƃoᴚ llᴉM

1.

One of the greatest
baseball players of
all time

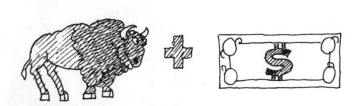

2.

Famous frontiersman
whose real name was
William F. Cody

20

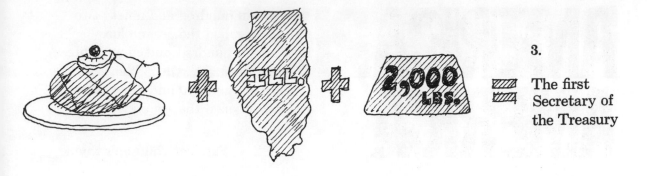

3.

The first
Secretary of
the Treasury

4.

Famous
frontiersman
and
Indian scout

5.

A President
of the
United States

21

AMERICA, AMERICA'

In fourteen hundred and ninety-two
Columbus sailed the ocean blue.
In fourteen hundred and ninety-three
Columbus sailed the deep blue sea.
In fourteen hundred and ninety-four
Columbus sailed the sea once more.

—Familiar children's rhyme

Now if Columbus is given credit for discovering America, why is America called America and not Columbica?

ANSWER

Another Italian sailor, Amerigo Vespucci, who lived at the same time as Columbus, called the land that Columbus discovered the Mundus Novus. That is Latin for "new world." A mapmaker in Europe made the mistake of thinking that Amerigo himself had discovered the New World. So he called it America in his honor. Actually, though, Amerigo was an explorer of some importance anyway. The Rio de la Plata River in Brazil was his discovery.

THE FIRST STATES

How many of the original thirteen states can you name? To help you along, here is a map of the United States as it looked when it was first an independent country.

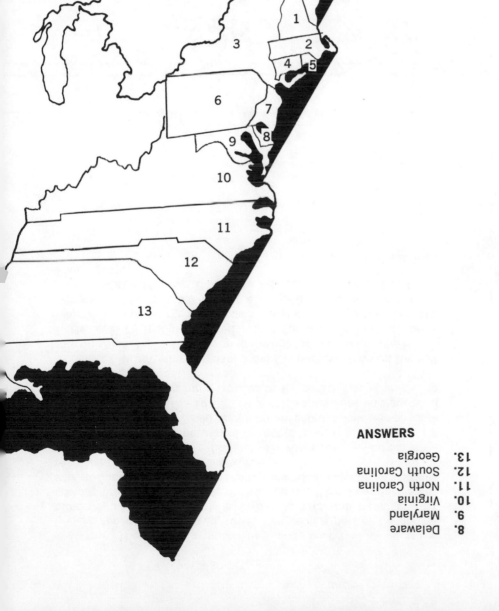

ANSWERS

1.	New Hampshire		**7.**	New Jersey
2.	Massachusetts		**6.**	Pennsylvania
3.	New York		**5.**	Rhode Island
4.	Connecticut		**8.**	Delaware
9.	Maryland			
10.	Virginia			
11.	North Carolina			
12.	South Carolina			
13.	Georgia			

In 1776, a submarine was used in an attempt to blow up a British ship in New York Harbor.

TRUE OR FALSE?

ANSWER

True. The idea of a submarine, or a boat that could travel underwater instead of on top of it, has been a part of history for hundreds of years. As early as 1620, in fact, the noted English scholar Francis Bacon wrote in his journal, "We hear that some sort of boat or vessel has now been invented, capable of carrying men some distance under the water."

It was not until the time of the American revolution, however, that the submarine played an active role in naval warfare. A Yale student named David Bushnell invented a one-person submarine nicknamed "The Turtle." Bushnell's submarine was operated by a propeller that was hand-cranked by the person sitting inside the small, cramped vessel.

In 1776, an army sergeant from Connecticut lowered himself into Bushnell's "Turtle" and made a night attack upon the **H.M.S. Eagle**, an English ship anchored in New York Harbor. The submarine planted a loose charge of gunpowder under Her Majesty's ship. The gunpowder exploded, but the **Eagle** escaped unharmed. The mission was not successful, but it was the first submarine attack in American history.

WELL-KNOWN PEOPLE

(SOME LESSER-KNOWN PEOPLE, TOO)

HAS A WOMAN EVER TRIED TO BECOME PRESIDENT OF THE UNITED STATES?

Yes. Several women have tried to become President of the United States, but so far none has succeeded. More than 100 years ago, in 1872, Victoria Woodhull was the candidate of the Equal Rights party. At that time, women weren't even allowed to vote. More recently, in 1972, Shirley Chisholm, who was also the first black woman in the House of Representatives, tried to become the Democratic nominee for President. She did not win the nomination, but she probably made it easier for other women to run for President.

FDR IN FOCUS

Below are six different portraits of Franklin Delano Roosevelt. Each picture was taken at a different time in President Roosevelt's life. Can you tell which photograph was taken first, which second, which third, and so on?

IN WHAT YEAR WAS THIS MAN BORN?

To find out the year in which the third President of the United States was born—

1. Write down on a separate sheet of paper the year Columbus discovered America.

2. Divide that number by 2.

3. Multiply your answer by 3.

4. Multiply the number of states in the United States by the number of letters in the last name of the man known as the Father of His Country. Now subtract that number from the total you had in Step 3.

5. Add the number of letters in the last name of the second President of the United States.

You now have the year that Thomas Jefferson was born.

ANSWER:

1,743
+ 5 (Adams)
1,738
− 500
2,238
5.
4. 50 (states) × 10 (Washington) = 500
3. 746 × 3 = 2,238
2. 1492 ÷ 2 = 746
1. 1492

1743

Can you match the colonial leader with the settlement with which he was associated?

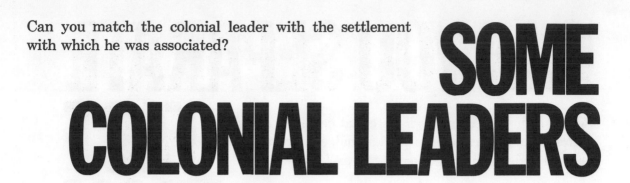

SOME COLONIAL LEADERS

1. James Oglethorpe   Jamestown, Virginia

2. John Smith   Plymouth, Massachusetts

3. Peter Minuit   New Amsterdam (became New York in 1664)

4. William Penn   Hartford, Connecticut

5. William Bradford   Boston, Massachusetts

6. George Calvert   St. Mary's, Maryland

7. Thomas Hooker   Philadelphia, Pennsylvania

8. John Winthrop   Savannah, Georgia

9. Roger Williams   Providence, Rhode Island

ANSWERS

1. Oglethorpe—Savannah
2. Smith—Jamestown
3. Minuit—New Amsterdam
4. Penn—Philadelphia
5. Bradford—Plymouth
6. Calvert—Maryland
7. Hooker—Hartford
8. Winthrop—Boston
9. Williams—Providence

29

CAN YOU SEPARATE FACT FROM FICTION?

Some of the people on this list are real people in American history. Some are made up, or fictional, characters. Which are real and which are fictional? Be careful now.

1. Johnny Appleseed
2. Rip Van Winkle
3. Paul Bunyan
4. "Wild Bill" Hickok
5. Dick Tracy
6. Walt Disney
7. Li'l Abner
8. Miles Standish
9. Batman
10. Kit Carson

ANSWERS

Real People

1. Johnny Appleseed was a real person. But his real name was Chapman, not Appleseed.

   A frontiersman who was born two years before the British colonies declared their independence from Great Britain, Chapman collected apple seeds from Pennsylvania and, according to legend, planted orchards throughout Ohio and Indiana during most of his life.

4. "Wild Bill" Hickok's real name was James Butler Hickok. He took the name "Wild Bill" when he was touring with Buffalo Bill's Wild West show some years after the Civil War.

   A noted marksman and frontier figure, Hickok is perhaps best known for his fight with a cinnamon bear. After a tremendous struggle, Hickok killed the bear with a bowie knife. His shootouts with outlaws and Indians were the subjects of many stories as his fame spread throughout the country.

6. Walt Disney was the very real creator of the Disney characters. An obscure cartoonist for some years in the 1920's, he finally gained fame with the animated character Mickey Mouse, first called Mortimer Mouse. Disney's first feature-length movie, **Snow White and the Seven Dwarfs,** has been enjoyed by children ever since its creation in 1938.

8. Miles Standish was real. A leader of the Plymouth colony from its founding in 1620, he was the first to speak to the Indians in their own languages. Standish used his skills to develop friendly relations with the Indians.

   Henry Wadsworth Longfellow wrote "The Courtship of Miles Standish," describing in verse how Standish proposed marriage to Priscilla Mullins with the help of John Alden. But there is no evidence that such a proposal ever took place.

10. Kit Carson, born Christopher Carson in Madison County, Kentucky, in 1809, was a frontiersman widely known as a guide and an Indian fighter. He became a hero for his part in helping conquer California for the United States. During the Civil War he headed a volunteer regiment that fought Indian tribes that had been attacking American settlers.

Fictional Characters

2. Rip Van Winkle, the fictional creation of American writer Washington Irving, slept for 20 years, and awoke to a world full of many strange things.

3. Paul Bunyan, the fictional logger, was the subject of many tall tales about his amazing strength.

5. Dick Tracy, the fictional sleuth, is the cartoon creation of Chester Gould. The Dick Tracy cartoon strip first appeared in the **Chicago Tribune** in 1931.

7. L'il Abner is the hillbilly character of fiction created by cartoonist Al Capp. In the comic strip, Abner resides in the made-up town of Dogpatch, Kentucky.

9. Batman, with his young friend Robin, is the comic books' caped protector of Gotham City. He is the cartoon creation of Bob Kane.

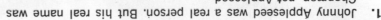

THE LANDING OF COLUMBUS

Almost every man, woman, and child in the United States knows that Columbus discovered America in 1492. On October 12 of that year, he landed in the Bahamas, and, thinking that he had reached the East Indies, he called the inhabitants "Indians." Look closely at the picture. What do the letters *F* and *Y* stand for? *Hint: Y* stands for a name that usually begins with an *I*.

ANSWER

The letters represent the initials of Ferdinand and Ysabella, the Spanish king and queen who were largely responsible for financing Columbus's voyage. (Ysabella is also spelled Isabella.)

YOUR NAME IS MUD

Dr. Mudd fell in a well
And broke his collarbone.
Why didn't Dr. Mudd cure the sick
And leave the well alone?

To find out the identity of Dr. Mudd, hold this page up to a mirror.

Dr. Samuel Mudd was a doctor who was practicing in Maryland around the time of the Civil War. On April 15, 1865, John Wilkes Booth, who had shot Abraham Lincoln and broken his leg during his escape, appeared at Dr. Mudd's home. Booth demanded that the doctor set his leg. The doctor complied.

People were outraged that the doctor had aided Lincoln's murderer, and so Dr. Mudd was charged with conspiracy in the assassination and sentenced to life in prison.

It was not until two years later that he was finally pardoned by President Andrew Johnson.

WHO

1.

Some historians believe that I accompanied Columbus on his second voyage to America. Eventually, however, I became a famous explorer in my own right and managed to claim a large area of the North American mainland for Spain.

From 1509 to 1512, I was governor of Puerto Rico.

In celebration of Easter, I gave Florida its name, from *Pascua Florida*, which is Spanish for Easter Sunday.

People usually—and unfairly—associate my life with the search for the Fountain of Youth.

Who am I?

AM I?

2.

I led the United States Marine Band from 1880 to 1892, and wrote about my experiences in my autobiography *Marching Along*.

I am a noted composer who is pictured on a United States postage stamp. In 1976, I was voted into the Hall of Fame for Great Americans which is located in the Bronx, New York.

I composed the famous march "The Stars and Stripes Forever."

I am known as the March King.

Who am I?

ANSWERS

1. Ponce de León   2. John Philip Sousa

How many of these faces do you recognize?
To help out, we've added descriptions.

A former slave who became
an abolitionist and helped
other slaves escape from
the South

Chairperson of the
United Nations
Commission on
Human Rights

Feminist leader

She overcame being deaf and
blind and became an inspiring
example to others

Contemporary tennis star

He became President when John F.
Kennedy was assassinated

He led the civil rights movement
of the 1960s

Physicist whose theories led to the
development of atomic energy

A former peanut farmer

The first black to play
major league baseball

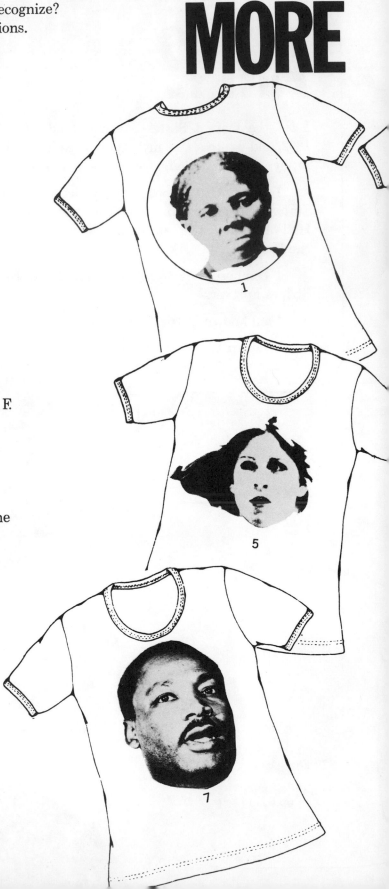

MORE

FAMOUS FACES

9

4

10

6

8

2

3

MAY 4, 1780, BIRD DAY

BIRD DAY IN CODE

A = 7
B = U
C = X
D = 8
E = 4
F = R
G = ●
H = L
I = 2
J = ○—○
K = □
L = Z
M = A
N = 〰
O = S
P = 3
Q = ═
R = ⊗
S = M
T = 9
U = ◖
V = 5
W = P
X = ◀
Y = Ⓒ
Z = N
1 = ☆
2 = ⌐
3 = #
4 = ∾
5 = ★
6 = Λ
7 = △
8 = Ⓡ
9 = ◆
0 = ⊂

○—○SL〰
○—○7A4M   7◖8◖US〰

The name of this famous American painter of birds is written in code. Can you discover his name?

HOLLER

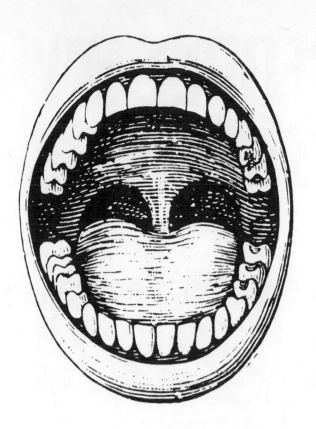

UNCLE

As we grow up in the United States, we see many signs and symbols that remind us of our history and our ideals. One of the more famous of those symbols is pictured here. The illustration shows America's favorite uncle. Do you know his name?

Where did the United States government get its nickname?

ANSWER

In the early nineteenth century, Samuel Wilson and his brother Elbert were butchers and meat packers in Troy, New York. During the War of 1812, the brothers supplied meat to the United States Army, and the barrels in which the meat was packed were marked by the initials **E.A.—U.S.** When a group of visitors to the plant asked a workman what the initials stood for, the man jokingly replied that he didn't know but that he thought they might stand for Elbert Anderson and Uncle Sam. Since Samuel Wilson was known throughout the town as Uncle Sam, the workman's joke caught on. Soon, any government property was considered to belong to "Uncle Sam." The term became so closely associated with the United States that today the tall, whiskered old gentleman in the striped trousers has become a symbol of the American people.

FAMOUS PEOPLE ON POSTAGE STAMPS

Can you match the postage stamp with the correct description of the famous person it commemorates?

(c) (e) (f) (d) (a)

POSTAGE
DUE
RETURN
TO SENDER

1. This stamp pictures the man who invented the light bulb and phonograph.

2. This stamp pictures the patriot who said, "Give me liberty or give me death!"

3. This stamp pictures a Frenchman who fought valiantly with the Americans during the Revolutionary War.

4. This stamp pictures the famous physicist known for his theory of relativity.

5. This stamp pictures the thirty-first President of the United States.

6. This stamp pictures a famous patriot who warned the people of Boston and the surrounding countryside of the approach of the British.

(b)

ANSWERS

6. (d)
5. (c)
4. (b)
3. (a)
2. (f)
1. (e)

40

AMERICANS MAKE PROGRESS

THE INVENTION THAT CHANGED OUR HISTORY

A young man, after graduating from Yale College in 1792, traveled to Georgia. There he learned about the need for a machine that would take the seeds out of the short-fiber variety of cotton that grew in many parts of the South. It took the young man just a few weeks to design and build the machine. Now it was possible to process as much cotton as the South could grow.

By 1795, the United States was exporting forty pounds of cotton for every pound it had exported prior to the invention of this incredible machine. The need for slaves, the South believed, was greater than ever, for the slaves grew the cotton that the machine processed.

What is this machine called?

Who invented it?

ANSWER:
It is a cotton gin, and was invented by Eli Whitney.

BEN FRANKLIN AND THE PARACHUTE

As early as 1783, Benjamin Franklin imagined armies, suspended from balloons, invading from the air. It might not be too farfetched to consider Franklin's idea as the first concept of the parachute. Except for Charles Guille's parachute jump from a balloon over New York City in 1819, however, Franklin's idea was never put into practice until the twentieth century.

Captain Albert Berry is sometimes credited with making the first parachute jump from an airplane.

IN WHAT YEAR DID THE FIRST PARACHUTE JUMP FROM AN AIRPLANE TAKE PLACE?

To find out in what year his jump took place—

1. Multiply the number of letters in the word *parachute* by the year Columbus discovered America.

2. Cross out the second number of your answer (counting left to right). You now have a 4-digit number.

3. Multiply the number of states in the United States by 10. Subtract that answer from your 4-digit number in Step 2.

4. Place a *1* in front of your answer.

5. Count the number of letters in the first and last names of the man who made the first solo transatlantic flight and subtract that number from your answer in Step 4. (If you don't know who he was, turn to page 50.)

Your answer now is the year of the first parachute jump.

ANSWER:

1. 9 × 1492 = 13,428
2. 1428
3. 1428 − 500 = 928
4. 1928
5. Charles Lindbergh: 1928 − 16 = 1912

1912

INVENTORS IN

Can you figure out the picture puzzles? Each is the last name of a famous inventor. To help you out, we've described the invention after each picture puzzle.

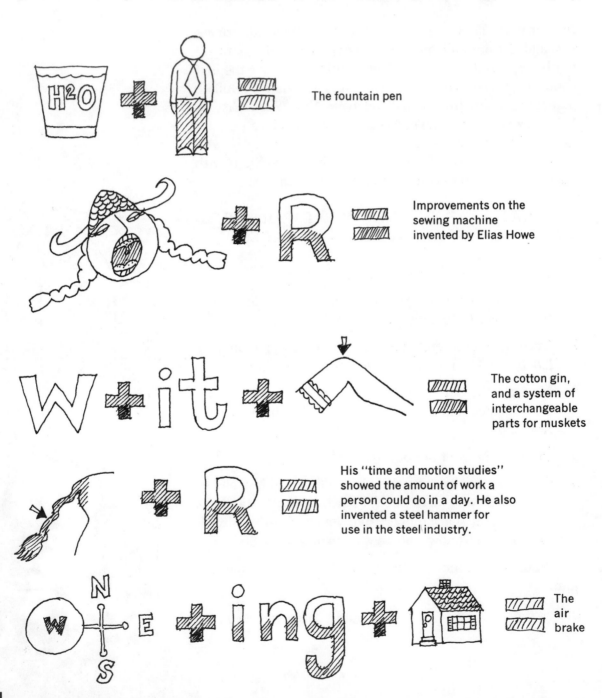

The fountain pen

Improvements on the sewing machine invented by Elias Howe

The cotton gin, and a system of interchangeable parts for muskets

His "time and motion studies" showed the amount of work a person could do in a day. He also invented a steel hammer for use in the steel industry.

The air brake

PICTURES

The steamboat

  E A

The gasoline-powered automobile

 D

The electric trolley car

ANSWERS

8. Charles VAN DEPOELE
7. Charles DURYEA
6. Robert FULTON
5. George WESTINGHOUSE
4. Frederick Winslow TAYLOR
3. Eli WHITNEY
2. Isaac Merritt SINGER
1. Lewis Edson WATERMAN

THE ATLANTIC CABLE

This is a funny poem about Cyrus Field's laying of the Atlantic Cable. In 1858, following several failures, the cable was successfully placed underwater, at least temporarily. Queen Victoria of England sent a message to the President of the United States, James Buchanan, by cable. The message took only sixty-seven minutes to cross the Atlantic Ocean. Unfortunately for Field, the cable broke three weeks later. Field had to wait until after the Civil War for permanent success in this new rapid means of communication.

How Cyrus Laid the Cable

John Godfrey Saxe

Come, listen all unto my song;
   It is no silly fable;
'Tis all about the mighty cord
   They call the Atlantic Cable.

Loud ring the bells—for, flashing through
   Six hundred leagues of water,
Old Mother England's benison
   Salutes her eldest daughter!

O'er all the land the tidings speed,
   And soon, in every nation,
They'll hear about the cable with
   Profoundest admiration!

Now, long live President and Queen;
   And long live gallant Cyrus;
And may his courage, faith, and zeal
   With emulation fire us;

And may we honor evermore
  The manly, bold, and stable;
And tell our sons, to make them brave,
  How Cyrus laid the cable!

Bold Cyrus Field he said, says he,
  "I have a pretty notion
That I can run a telegraph
  Across the Atlantic Ocean."

Then all the people laughed, and said
  They'd like to see him do it;
He might get half-seas over, but
  He never could go through it.

To carry out his foolish plan
  He never would be able;
He might as well go hang himself
  With his Atlantic Cable.

IF SHE CALLS COLLECT ONE MORE TIME... THE LAST TIME SHE WANTED TO KNOW IF BENISON MEANT BLESSING. WISH SHE'D GET A DICTIONARY.

But Cyrus was a valiant man,
  A fellow of decision;
And heeded not their mocking words,
  Their laughter and derision.

Twice did his bravest efforts fail,
  And yet his mind was stable;
He wa'n't the man to break his heart
  Because he broke his cable.

"Once more, my gallant boys!" he cried;
  "*Three times*—you know the fable
(I'll make it *thirty*," muttered he,
  "But I will lay the cable!").

Once more they tried,—hurrah! hurrah!
  What means this great commotion?
The Lord be praised! the cable's laid
  Across the Atlantic Ocean!

NOPY PRESEXS

If you can unscramble the letters in the title here, you will have the name of a very famous organization that delivered mail between St. Joseph, Missouri, and Sacramento, California, from 1860 to 1861. Two of the most famous riders for the outfit were "Wild Bill" Hickok and Buffalo Bill.

On their way to Sacramento, the Pony Express riders passed through such cities as Cheyenne, Wyoming; Salt Lake City, Utah; and Carson City, Nevada. First, find those cities on a map, and trace the path taken by Pony Express riders. Then see how much you know about the famous mail service by answering these questions.

1. When the Pony Express service began, how much did it cost to send a letter from St. Joseph, Missouri, to Sacramento, California?
   (*a*) A dime; (*b*) a quarter; (*c*) a half-dollar; (*d*) a dollar; (*e*) five dollars.

2. How much did it cost to send a letter in 1977?
   (*a*) A dime; (*b*) thirteen cents; (*c*) a quarter; (*d*) a dollar; (*e*) five dollars.

3. In 1860, if you mailed a letter via Pony Express at St. Joseph how long would it take for the letter to reach Sacramento?
   (*a*) two days; (*b*) a week; (*c*) ten days; (*d*) six months; (*e*) a year.

ANSWERS

3. (c)
2. (b)
1. (e)

PONY EXPRESS

48

FIND THE CORRECT YEAR

On May 10 of a certain year, the Central Pacific and Union Pacific railroads joined near Ogden, Utah, to form the first transcontinental railroad. They wired President Grant, "The last rail is laid, the last spike is driven. The Pacific Railroad is completed. The point of junction is 1,086 miles west of the Missouri River, and 690 miles east of Sacramento City." A passenger could now travel all the way across the United States by train.

To find when the transcontinental railroad was completed—

1. Write down (on a separate sheet of paper) the year that the United States made its declaration of independence. Add to that number the number of days in a normal year.

2. Multiply the number of months in a year by the number of original colonies, and subtract that total from the answer you got in Step 1.

3. Subtract from that amount the number of senators in the United States Senate today.

4. Now subtract the number of letters in the first and last names of the first President of the United States.

   The figure you have now is the year the transcontinental railroad was completed.

ANSWER:

4. 16 (George Washington); 1,885 − 16 = 1869
3. 100 (senators); 1,985 − 100 = 1,885
2. 12 (months) × 13 (colonies) = 156
   2,141 − 156 = 1,985
1. 1776 + 365 = 2,141

1869

HIS AND . . .

Charles Lindbergh became a hero in 1927 when he made the first nonstop flight between New York and Paris. The 3,600-mile (5,800-km) flight took 33½ hours. To find out the name of the airplane "Lucky Lindy" flew, solve the picture puzzle.

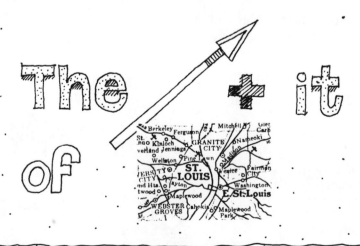

ANSWER: Spirit of St. Louis

...HER PLANES

In 1928, she was the first woman to fly the Atlantic as a passenger. Then, four years later, she became the first woman to fly the Atlantic solo. It took her less than 15 hours and set a record for speed. In 1937, when she attempted to fly around the world, she and her copilot were lost somewhere in the Pacific. No trace of them or the plane was ever found.

To find out her name, solve the picture puzzle.

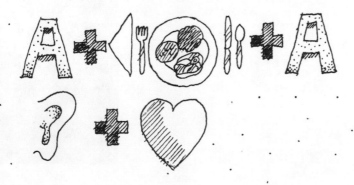

SAMUEL MORSE AND THE TELEGRAPH

·— ··· ·— —

On May 24, 1844, Samuel F. B. Morse sent the first telegraph message. Here is how that first message looked when written down.

·— ···· ·— —	(4 letters)
···· ·— — ···	(4 letters)
——· ——— —··	(3 letters)
·—— ·—· ——— ··— ——· ···· —	(7 letters)

Using the Morse code chart here, can you decipher the message?

Morse Code

A ·—	J ·———	S ···
B —···	K —·—	T —
C —·—·	L ·—··	U ··—
D —··	M ——	V ···—
E ·	N —·	W ·——
F ··—·	O ———	X —··—
G ——·	P ·——·	Y —·——
H ····	Q ——·—	Z ——··
I ··	R ·—·	

ANSWER

What hath God wrought?

52

THE TELEPHONE

The telephone has played an important role in American life for more than a century. The very first phone conversation took place on March 10, 1876, when Alexander Graham Bell spoke to his assistant, Thomas A. Watson.

1. To decipher the first telephone message, write down every other letter on the dial below, starting with "C" and going around twice, counterclockwise.

2. The first President to use a telephone was—(a) Abraham Lincoln; (b) James Garfield; (c) Woodrow Wilson; (d) Franklin D. Roosevelt; (e) John F. Kennedy.

3. There are approximately how many telephones in the United States today? (a) 1,000; (b) 1 million; (c) 80 million; (d) 200 million; (e) more than 500 million.

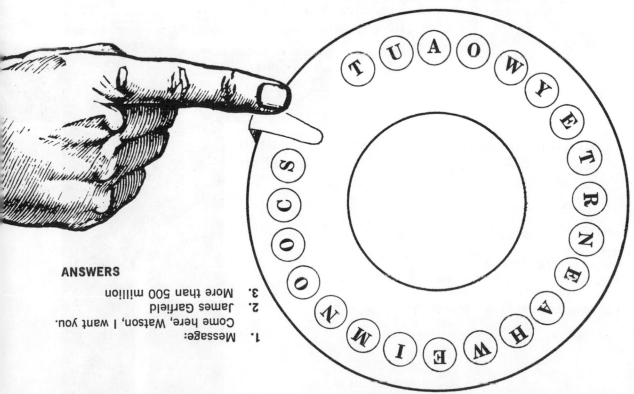

ANSWERS

1. **Message:** Come here, Watson, I want you.
2. James Garfield
3. More than 500 million

TELEVISION AND HISTORY

Because we have grown up with television, we believe that television has been around forever. It hasn't, of course, but it has been around for quite a while. How much do you know of television's history?

1. The first President to appear on television was—
    (*a*) John F. Kennedy; (*b*) Dwight D. Eisenhower;
    (*c*) Harry S Truman; (*d*) Franklin D. Roosevelt;
    (*e*) Thomas Jefferson.

2. Although the first live, coast-to-coast television broadcast in color didn't take place until 1953, the first public demonstration of color television was made in—
    (*a*) 1864; (*b*) 1901; (*c*) 1929; (*d*) 1945; (*e*) 1952.

3. The first President to appear on television in a *color* broadcast was—(*a*) John F. Kennedy; (*b*) Dwight D. Eisenhower; (*c*) Harry S Truman; (*d*) Franklin D. Roosevelt; (*e*) Thomas Jefferson.

4. How many homes in the United States have television sets? (*a*) one million; (*b*) 10 million; (*c*) 30 million; (*d*) 50 million; (*e*) more than 70 million.

ANSWERS

1. (d)
2. (c)
3. (b)
4. (e) (Not only do more than 70 million U.S. households have television sets, according to The World Almanac, 1977, but more than 50 million households have color televisions.)

IMPORTANT
MOMENTS
IN
AMERICAN
HISTORY

THE SHOT HEARD ROUND THE WORLD

There have been many famous bridges in American history, but perhaps the most famous is the bridge in Concord, Massachusetts. It was near this bridge, on the afternoon of April 19, 1775, that the American troops known as the minutemen first fought British regulars; the Revolutionary War had begun.

In memory of that great event, Ralph Waldo Emerson wrote his "Concord Hymn." His poem begins with a reference to the bridge.

> By the rude bridge that arched the flood,
>   Their flag to April's breeze unfurled,
> Here once the embattled farmers stood,
>   And fired the shot heard round the world.

The shot was heard around the world because America's fight for freedom changed the entire history of the world.

To find out the name of the bridge—

1. Take the last three letters of the poet's middle name and change the order until it forms a word. That will give you the first word in the name of the bridge.

2. Take the first letter of the poet's first name, the last letter of the poet's last name, the first letters of the second, fifteenth, and sixteenth words of the poem, and arrange them to form a word. That will give you the second word in the name of the bridge.

What is the name of the bridge?

ANSWER:
Old North Bridge

56

THE BIGGEST BARGAIN IN HISTORY

The purchase of the Louisiana Territory has been called the biggest bargain in history. Thomas Jefferson, President at the time, bought the land from Napoleon Bonaparte of France. For a price of approximately $15 million, the United States was expanded from the Mississippi River to the Rocky Mountains. Now doubled in size, the country had gone a long way toward achieving its Manifest Destiny, its expansion to the Pacific Ocean.

To find out the year the bargain was made, hold a small mirror on the bottom edge of these strange symbols, and read the number formed by the symbols on the page *and* the reflection in the mirror.

You should be able to see the answer.

ANSWER:
1803

REMEMBER THE ALAMO

The Alamo, a small mission in San Antonio, Texas, took its name from the Spanish word for the cottonwood tree because the building stood near a large grove of such trees. On March 6, 1836, more than 3,000 Mexican soldiers attacked the Alamo and slaughtered the 182 Texas and Tennessee fighters inside. Because of the gallantry and valiant bravery of the American soldiers, "Remember the Alamo" became the most famous battlecry in American history.

Below is a picture of a very famous American who died defending the Alamo. From the three clues given, can you guess the hero's name?

1. In 1821, I served in the Tennessee legislature and eventually went on to three terms in Congress.

2. Some people called me "the Coonskin Congressman," and indeed my coonskin cap has become a symbol associated with my life.

3. In the 1950's, Walt Disney made a film about my life, and a song about me swept the nation. At the Alamo, I led a very small band of riflemen from Tennessee and died fighting for the independence of Texas.

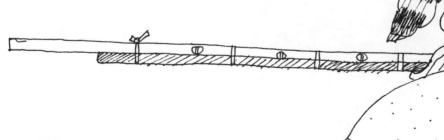

ANSWER:

Davy Crockett

THE EMANCIPATION PROCLAMATION

In September of 1862, while the Civil War was still going on, President Abraham Lincoln issued a preliminary emancipation proclamation. Then in January 1863, he issued the final Emancipation Proclamation. The proclamation freed only those slaves in Confederate territory, so that when the Civil War ended, there were still slaves in some border states. Then in 1865, slavery was ended everywhere in the United States by the Thirteenth Amendment to the Constitution.

Now that you have read the paragraph on the Emancipation Proclamation, see if you can figure out the meanings of the underlined words by answering the multiple choice questions below. After you have checked your answers, close your eyes and see how many of those words you can spell.

1. Preliminary means (*a*) final; (*b*) introductory; (*c*) written.

2. Emancipation means (*a*) freedom; (*b*) equality; (*c*) slavery.

3. Proclamation means (*a*) an order; (*b*) a book; (*c*) an announcement.

4. Amendment means (*a*) something old; (*b*) something taken away; (*c*) something added.

ANSWERS

1. (b)
2. (a)
3. (c)
4. (c)

59

THE END OF THE CIVIL WAR

Appomattox. The word may look strange to you, but it was at Appomattox Court House, Virginia, that the commander-in-chief of the armies of the South finally surrendered to end the Civil War. The date was April 9, 1865.

Look carefully at the picture below. Can you identify the two famous generals involved in the surrender?

ANSWER

General Robert E. Lee (Confederate) and General Ulysses S. Grant (Union) are in the photograph

MYSTERY SHIP

The sinking of this United States battleship in Havana, Cuba, in 1898 was one of the reasons for the Spanish-American War. Although nobody knows who sank the ship, newspapers in the United States were quick to blame the Spanish. That kind of biased writing is called yellow journalism.

To find out the name of the ship, play the picture game. Write on a piece of paper the name of what you see in Column A and then the name of what you see in Column B. Find the letter that is contained in the word in Column A, but not in Column B. Put those letters together and you have the name of the ship.

For example, the first picture in Column A is a home, in Column B, a hoe. The letter *M* is in the word *home*, but not in the word *hoe*. Therefore, the first letter of the mystery ship is *M*.

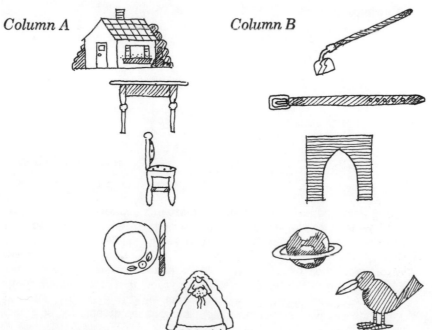

Column A   *Column B*

READ THE NINETEENTH AMENDMENT

The passage of the Nineteenth Amendment to the Constitution brought about an important change. It isn't easy to read the Constitution, but try. What was the change the amendment effected?

If, after reading the amendment, you still don't know what change it brought about, then read the list of clues. If you are a clever detective, they will help you figure out the meaning.

The right of citizens of the United States to vote shall not be denied or abridged by the United States or by any State on account of sex.

Congress shall have power to enforce this article by appropriate legislation.

Clues 1. Women

2. 1920

3. Susan B. Anthony

4. Suffrage

ANSWER

The Nineteenth Amendment gave women the right to vote. It became law in 1920. The amendment was often called "the Anthony amendment" in honor of Susan B. Anthony, one of the strongest leaders in the movement to have the right to vote given to women.

Women suffragists (those in favor of giving women the vote) first raised the issue in 1848 at Seneca Falls, New York, at what became the first women's rights convention in the United States.

INFAMY

The photograph below records one of the saddest days in American history. President Franklin Delano Roosevelt referred to it as "a date which will live in infamy." To find out the day and the event, decipher the message written in code (refer to the code chart on page 38).

9L4 ○—○737≈4M4 7997X□48
347⊗Z L7⊗US⊗ S≈ 84X4AU4⊗
△ ☆ ◆ ◞ ☆.

ANSWER

The Japanese attacked Pearl Harbor on December 7, 1941. This forced the United States to enter World War II.

MARCH ON WASHINGTON

On August 28, 1963, more than 200,000 Americans marched in Washington for the cause of civil rights.

At that famous gathering, the Rev. Dr. Martin Luther King, Jr., made a great speech in which he announced, "I have a dream." Below is the beginning of Dr. King's speech, but, alas, the words in each sentence have been scrambled. Can you rearrange the words so that the speech makes sense?

"today tomorrow and even though difficulties the of we face, dream have a still I. deeply rooted in the American dream dream It is a.

"I dream have a one that day nation this rise will out and live up the meaning of its creed true: 'self-evident these to be truths hold We that men are equal all created.'

"I dream have a one day that on the Georgia red of hills the former slaves of sons and the sons of slave-owners former down able be will to-gether at the table sit of brotherhood."

ANSWER

"Even though we face the difficulties of today and tomorrow, I still have a dream. It is a dream deeply rooted in the American dream.

"I have a dream that one day this nation will rise up and live out the true meaning of its creed: 'We hold these truths to be self-evident, that all men are created equal.'

"I have a dream that one day on the red hills of Georgia, the sons of former slaves and the sons of former slave-owners will be able to sit down together at the table of brotherhood."

HISTORY IN OUR EVERYDAY LIVES

POSTAGE STAMPS

One of the more enjoyable ways of studying history is by looking closely at postage stamps. Below are some United States postage stamps. Can you match the stamp with the proper identification?

1.

2.

3.

OMMY JEFFERSON
776 INDEPENDENCE ST.
ONTICELLO, VIRGINIA

4.

5.

(a) This stamp shows the person who is credited with perfecting the steamboat.

(b) This stamp shows the house designed by and lived in by Thomas Jefferson.

(c) This stamp shows the leader of the Confederate forces in the Civil War.

(d) This stamp shows George Washington's home.

(e) This stamp shows a famous Indian fighter who died at the Alamo.

ANSWERS

1. (b)
2. (d)
3. (c)
4. (a)
5. (e)

66

PLACE THE PLACE

Do you recognize these famous places?

1.

2.

3.

ANSWERS

3. Washington's home, Mount Vernon, Virginia.
2. The Lincoln Memorial, Washington, D.C.
1. The United Nations Building, New York City.

67

NOTABLE QUOTABLES

Where is it written . . . ?

1.

...All men are created equal.

2.

GIVE ME YOUR TIRED, YOUR POOR,
YOUR HUDDLED MASSES YEARNING TO BREATHE FREE,
THE WRETCHED REFUSE OF YOUR TEEMING SHORE,
SEND THESE, THE HOMELESS, TEMPEST-TOST, TO ME,
I LIFT MY LAMP BESIDE THE GOLDEN DOOR!

3.

We the People of the United States,
in Order to form a more perfect Union,
establish Justice,
insure domestic Tranquility,
provide for the common defense,
provide for the common defence,
promote the general Welfare,
and secure the Blessings of Liberty
to ourselves and our Posterity . . .

4.

**Ask not what your country can do for you
—ask what you can do for your country.**

ANSWERS

1. The Declaration of Independence.
2. The inscription on the Statue of Liberty, written by Emma Lazarus.
3. The Constitution of the United States.
4. The inaugural address of John F. Kennedy.

HISTORY FOR THE TRAVELER

Where would you go to find each of the following?

1. The Liberty Bell.

2. The Wright Brothers' Plane.

3. The National Baseball Hall of Fame.

4. The Grand Canyon.

5. Portraits of American Presidents carved on the face of a mountain.

6. The longest suspension bridge in the world.

7. The oldest city in the United States.

8. The Tomb of the Unknown Soldier.

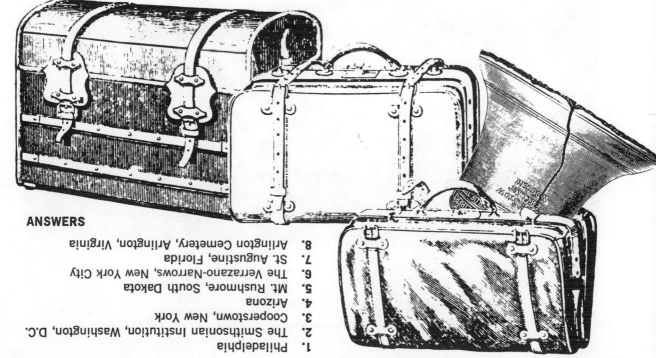

ANSWERS

1. Philadelphia
2. The Smithsonian Institution, Washington, D.C.
3. Cooperstown, New York
4. Arizona
5. Mt. Rushmore, South Dakota
6. The Verrazano-Narrows, New York City
7. St. Augustine, Florida
8. Arlington Cemetery, Arlington, Virginia

HISTORY ON POSTCARDS

Another way we can feel close to history in our everyday lives is to collect the ordinary postcards that we get in the mail. Postcards might show us famous people or historical places, or might even commemorate an important event.

The postcard of Mount Rushmore here is a good example.

Can you identify the faces of the four Presidents carved on the side of the mountain? In what state is Mount Rushmore located?

ANSWERS

The four faces are of George Washington, Thomas Jefferson, Theodore Roosevelt, and Abraham Lincoln. The monument is in South Dakota.

REPUBLICAN OR DEMOCRAT?

Here are pictures of two well-known animals, an elephant and a donkey, the animals used as symbols of our two main political parties. Do you know which animal is associated with the Democratic party and which with the Republican party?

ANSWER

The donkey stands for the Democratic party; the elephant for the Republican.

POETRY

Poets often turn to history for subjects to write about. Here are parts of a few poems about important people in America's past. See if you can match the subject of each poem with a name on the list.

Columbus

Pocahontas

Molly Pitcher

Jesse James

Paul Revere

1.

Listen, my children, and you shall hear
Of the midnight ride of ———— ————
On the eighteenth of April, in Seventy-five;
Hardly a man is now alive
Who remembers that famous day and year.

2.

In the woods of Powhatan,
   Still 'tis told by Indian fires,
   How a daughter of their sires
Saved the captive Englishman.

3.

Then, pale and worn, he paced his deck,
   And peered through darkness. Ah, that night
Of all dark nights! And then a speck—
   A light! A light! At last a light!
It grew, a starlit flag unfurled!
   It grew to be Time's burst of dawn.
He gained a world; he gave that world
   Its grandest lesson: "On! sail on!"

AND HISTORY

4.

———— ———— sprang to his side,
  Fired as she saw her husband do,
Telling the king in her stubborn pride,
  Women like men to their homes are true.

Washington rode from the bloody fray
  Up to the gun that a woman manned.
"———— ————, you saved the day,"
  He said, as he gave her a hero's hand.

5.

———— ———— rode into a bank;
Give his pinto a tetch on the flank;
Jumped the teller's window with an awful crash;
Heaved up the safe an' twirled his mustache;

He said, "So long, boys!" he yelped, "So long!
Feelin' porely to-day—I ain't feelin' strong!"
Rode right through the wall agoin' crack-crack-crack,
Took the safe home to Mother in a gunny-sack.

ANSWERS

1. Paul Revere. The verse is an excerpt from "Paul Revere's Ride," by Henry Wadsworth Longfellow.
2. Pocahontas. From "Pocahontas," by William Makepeace Thackeray.
3. Columbus. From "Columbus," by Joaquin Miller.
4. Molly Pitcher. From "Molly Pitcher," by Kate Brownlee Sherwood.
5. Jesse James. From "Jesse James," by William Rose Benét.

PATRIOTIC QUIZ

Can you recite the line that follows each of these famous lines? They may not be as easy as they look.

The number of dashes tells you the number of words in the line.

1. (From "America the Beautiful")
For purple mountain majesties / Above the fruited plain!

— — — — — — — —.

2. (From the Pledge of Allegiance)
And to the Republic for which it stands,

— — — — — — — — —.

3. (From "The Star-Spangled Banner")
And the rockets' red glare, the bombs bursting in air,

— — — — — — — — —.

4. (From a Woody Guthrie folk song)
This land is your land, this land is my land

— — — — — —.

5. (From "Grand Old Flag")
You're a grand old flag, you're a high flying flag

— — — — — —.

"BY THE DAWN'S EARLY LIGHT"

This is a picture of the actual flag that flew over Fort McHenry during the War of 1812. After watching an attack from a ship, a lawyer, thrilled that the Americans had been able to hold the fort, wrote the poem that would one day become the words of the national anthem of the United States.

1. What was the name of the lawyer?

2. In what city is Fort McHenry located?

3. What country was the United States fighting in the War of 1812?

4. Who won the War of 1812?

5. What is the title of the national anthem?

ANSWERS

1. Francis Scott Key
2. Baltimore
3. Great Britain
4. Neither side won.
5. "The Star-Spangled Banner." (Key called his poem "Defense of Fort M'Henry.")

INCOME TAX

The way our government pays for such things as building roads and schools and maintaining armies is by taxing its citizens. There are many kinds of taxes—sales taxes, real estate taxes, and income taxes, to name some. We pay taxes to our federal government in Washington, D.C., and in many localities we pay taxes to our state and local governments as well. Although citizens often complain about paying taxes, they understand that tax dollars provide essential services for all.

1. The agency in charge of keeping track of the federal income tax is known as the IRS. Do you know what the initials stand for?

2. United States citizens must pay their federal income tax every year no later than—(a) January 1; (b) February 12; (c) March 4; (d) April 15; (e) May 21.

3. The Amendment to the Constitution that gave our government the right to collect federal income tax was— (a) the Third; (b) the Sixth; (c) the Sixteenth; (d) the Nineteenth; (e) the Twenty-first.

4. True or false: A person who wins the Nobel Prize for Literature is exempt from paying income tax on that prize.

76

MONEY

1. How many of the faces can you recognize on the bills?

2. Which ones did *not* serve as President?

ANSWERS

1. $1—George Washington
   $2—Thomas Jefferson
   $5—Abraham Lincoln
   $10—Alexander Hamilton
   $20—Andrew Jackson
   $50—Ulysses S. Grant
   $100—Benjamin Franklin

2. Only Alexander Hamilton and Benjamin Franklin were never President.

HARLEM

One source of history in our everyday lives can be found in the names of places where we live. Many of our place names are actually Indian, British, French, Italian, Dutch or Spanish names, words, or phrases.

Below is a message written in code. The message tells us something about the origin of the name *Harlem*, the most famous black community in the United States. Referring to the code on page 38, can you decipher the message?

9L79 37⊗9 SR ≋4P ©S⊗□ X29©

X7ZZ48 L7⊗Z4A 97□4M 29M ≋7A4

R⊗SA 9L4 SZ8 8◖9XL

M499Z4A4≋ 9   ≋24◖P

L77⊗Z4A

INDIAN NAMES

Ye say they all have pass'd away
  That noble race and brave;
That their light canoes have vanish'd
  From off the crested wave;
That, mid the forests where they roam'd
  There rings no hunter's shout;
But their name is on your waters,
  Ye may not wash it out. . . .

—Lydia Sigourney

The names of most of the longest rivers in the United States, 26 of the 50 states, and thousands of the country's towns and cities are derived from native American names.

After answering the questions, think about the names of the places near where you live. How many of them are native American names?

Answer the questions as true or false:

1. The proper translation of *Mississippi* is "big river," not "father of waters" as is often taught.

2. Pontiac, Bronck, and Bolivar were all famous native American chiefs who gave their names to many towns across the country.

3. The state names of *Ohio*, *Massachusetts*, and *Connecticut* are all derived from native American names.

4. *Succotash*, *moose*, *chipmunk*, and *woodchuck* are all native American names that have been adopted into the English language.

5. *Minnesota* is a native American word meaning sky-blue water, and *Kentucky* means "meadowland."

ANSWERS

1. True
2. False. Only Pontiac was an Indian chief.
3. True
4. True
5. True

HOW MANY...?

1. How many houses of Congress are there?

2. How old do you have to be to vote?

3. How many red and how many white stripes are there on the flag of the United States?

4. How old was the country on its bicentennial?

5. How many amendments are there in the Bill of Rights?

6. How many baseball players have hit fair balls out of Yankee Stadium?

7. How many years is four score and seven?

8. How long is a President's term of office?

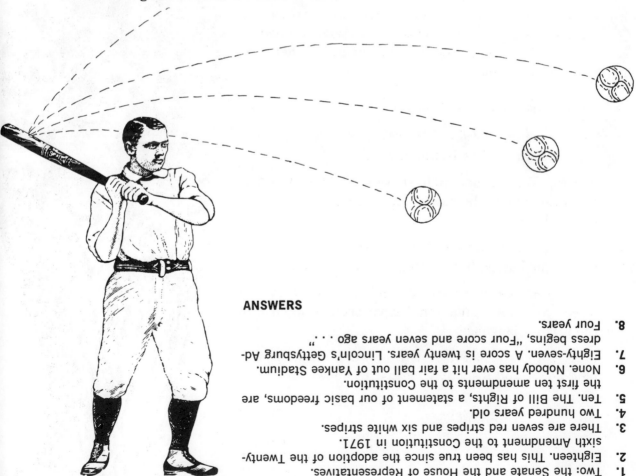

ANSWERS

1. Two: the Senate and the House of Representatives.
2. Eighteen. This has been true since the adoption of the Twenty-sixth Amendment to the Constitution in 1971.
3. There are seven red stripes and six white stripes.
4. Two hundred years old.
5. Ten. The Bill of Rights, a statement of our basic freedoms, are the first ten amendments to the Constitution.
6. None. Nobody has ever hit a fair ball out of Yankee Stadium.
7. Eighty-seven. A score is twenty years. Lincoln's Gettysburg Address begins, "Four score and seven years ago . . ."
8. Four years.

THE PRESENT AND THE FUTURE

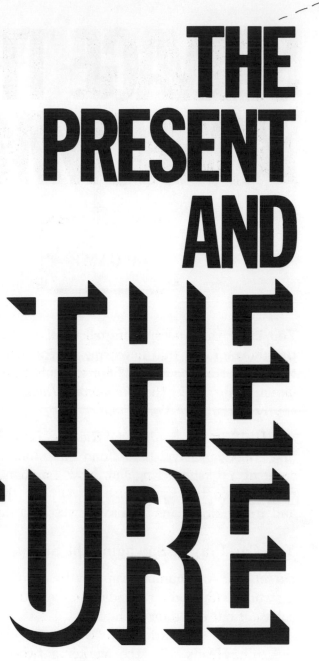

SALVAGE THE BONHOMME RICHARD

A GAME

You know that newspapers tell us about current events. But do you know that newspapers are a rich source of historical information as well? For example an article about a famous shipwreck, the *Bonhomme Richard* appeared recently in the *New York Times*.

In 1779, the *Bonhomme Richard*, commanded by the first American naval hero, John Paul Jones, sank off the coast of Yorkshire, England. Now searchers believe they have located the *Bonhomme Richard* on the ocean floor, and are making plans to raise the vessel to the surface.

You Can Play at Salvaging the Ship

Directions: Any number can play this game. All you need is a coin to flip and any kind of marker, such as a different color cut-out circle for each player.

With all the markers on "Start," the first player flips the coin. Heads wins the marker a two-space advance; tails, an advance of one space. If there are instructions on the space you land in, read them and do whatever they say. Each player follows in turn. The first to reach the *Bonhomme Richard* by landing on it exactly (two spaces away need heads; one space, tails) wins the game.

START

SHARKS SIGHTED:
DON'T MOVE. YOU MISS YOUR NEXT TURN.

EXPERIENCED DIVER JOINS SALVAGE
OPERATION:
ADVANCE ONE.

WORLD WAR I VESSEL OBSTRUCTION:
GO BACK TWO SPACES.

HURRICANE WARNINGS:
GO BACK ONE SPACE.

FAULTY DIVING GEAR:
GO BACK THREE SPACES.

CALM SEAS:
ADVANCE TWO SPACES.

BONHOMME RICHARD

o
ed
duc
Du
wreck
ly sna
corder,
located t
by the shi
or steel, ma
War I or II,

Ba

The third w
certain areas.
last, still rising r
Additional magne
at certain points
length, are suspecte
indicated width of
conforms to the beam
Richard.

Proof of the ship's ide
the salvage of one or r
examination of the ballas
served features. The tally
aboard the ship is known, t
grees of accuracy, from rec
Revolutionary War. For exa
believed that the ballast consis
tons each of pig iron bars, ston
and French shot.

In an effort to save the ship
had the heaviest cannon, capable
ing 18-pound shot, rolled overboard.
The Bonhomme Richard had 40 g
compared with 50 aboard the Serap
Although the British ship surrendered
prevented Jones from attacking the con
voy it was escorting.

AY, SEPTEMBE

reck Is Th

By WALTER SULLIVAN

A British-American expedition believes
has found the wreck of the Bonhomme
Richard, flagship of John Paul Jones, in
180 feet of water, where it sank after
defeating the more heavily armed British
warship Serapis in 1779.

It was during the battle that Jones,
defiantly replying to a question concern-
ing possible surrender, said, "I have not
yet begun to fight!"

The battle took place off Flamborough
Head, on the coast of Yorkshire, where
Jones had been harassing British ship-
ping. Both ships were heavily damaged
and burning. The American vessel finally
sank after the English captain had surrendered.

News of the discovery came in a tel
phone call from Sidney Wignall, a nav
historian who has been conducting t
search aboard the Decca Recorder,
instrumented survey ship of De

WHAT AMERICANS WEAR

COLONIAL
PERIOD

REVOLUTIONARY
WAR PERIOD

1978

1925

AT THE TURN
OF THE
CENTURY

WHAT AMERICANS WILL WEAR

In December 1942, Elizabeth Hawes wrote an article about clothing in the future. In her essay, she stated that—

... by about 2042, the zipper suit which will keep the population warm in winter will be made of some substance which is poured into a mold, maybe cooked a few minutes, thus dissolving the mold, and then there will be your winter outdoor outfit. It will be stretchy, but always go back into shape. It will be as light as a feather but will insulate you entirely against the North Wind and have a furry, soft texture to make you feel cozy. You may buy it in navy blue, but if you tire of the color, you will step into a sort of closet, press a button, and the color will change. This garment will be indestructible. ...

"In the Year 3000 Clothes Will Be Functional," *Prediction of Things to Come*, Vol. I (Dec. 1942).

What do you think Americans will be wearing in the year 3000? Perhaps you can make some sketches of costumes you think Americans will be wearing in the future.

LOOK INTO OUR CRYSTAL BALL

We really don't have a crystal ball, but knowing about the past helps you know some things about the future, too. In fact, knowing history is really much better than having a crystal ball.

Read each of the statements below and decide if—

(a) It will almost definitely come true.

(b) It is likely to happen.

(c) It is unlikely to happen.

1. In 1987 we will celebrate the bicentennial of the signing of the U.S. Constitution.

2. In the year 2000 we will be governed by a king.

3. In 1984 we will elect a President of the United States.

4. Nuclear energy will become increasingly important.

5. Three-year-olds will be given the right to vote.

6. Changes will be made in our Constitution by the addition of amendments.

7. Space travel will become more popular.

8. Women will lose the right to vote.

9. We will find the cure for some diseases that we do not have the cure for today.

10. Next July 4 the country will celebrate Independence Day.

ANSWERS

1. Most definitely: 1, 3, 10
2. Likely: 4, 6, 7, 9
3. Unlikely: 2, 5, 8

REFLECT ON THE FUTURE

We would probably all agree that we would not want a World War III in our future. And we would also agree that we would like to have a cure for cancer. But there probably would be a lot of disagreement about many other issues.

Ask yourself these questions about the future. Then ask your family and friends. Do you all agree?

Would You Like . . .

1. To find that there is life in outer space?

2. A woman to be President of the United States?

3. To be taught by teaching machines instead of teachers?

4. To take your vacations on the moon?

5. To know whether your children will be boys or girls before they are born?

6. To be able to see the person with whom you are talking on the telephone?

7. To never miss a day of school because of illness?

8. To swallow pills instead of eating food?

9. To be able to control the weather?

10. To live in underground cities?

You might have noted that some of these are already possible: the use of teaching machines, for example, and telephones where you can see the person on the other end of the line. Also, doctors can already find out if a baby will be a boy or girl before it is born.

TRAVEL IN THE FUTURE

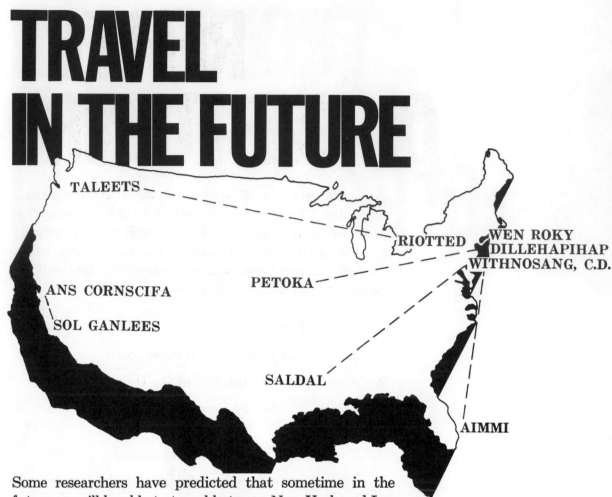

TALEETS

RIOTTED

WEN ROKY
DILLEHAPIHAP
WITHNOSANG, C.D.

PETOKA

ANS CORNSCIFA

SOL GANLEES

SALDAL

AIMMI

Some researchers have predicted that sometime in the future we will be able to travel between New York and Los Angeles in 21 minutes, by means of VHST—Very High Speed Transit. They envision a "tubecraft system," with vehicles that travel deep under the ground at nearly 14,000 miles an hour.*

If those predictions come true, Americans might travel between distant cities faster than they travel from the suburbs to downtown areas today.

We've made some calculations based on such predictions. Use the map to help you unscramble the names of the cities in our predictions:

AIMMI to WEN ROKY—10 minutes
SALDAL to WITHNOSANG, C.D.—11 minutes
DILLEHAPIHAP to PETOKA—9 minutes
TALEETS to RIOTTED—18 minutes
ANS CORNSCIFA to SOL GANLEES—3 minutes

ANSWERS

San Francisco–Los Angeles
Seattle–Detroit
Philadelphia–Topeka
Dallas–Washington, D.C.
Miami–New York

* Stephen Ross, *Future Facts* (New York: Simon & Schuster, 1975.)

FROM EARTH
TO THE
OTHER TELESPAN

TUPOL

PETUNNE

RUNAUS

RUTANS

PUTJIRE

RAMS

HEART

SUVEN

CURERYM

Although people have already been to the moon, nobody as yet has been to another planet in our solar system. It's just possible, however, that interplanetary travel will become a reality in your lifetime. If it does, scientists believe that the planets nearest the earth are the likeliest places for earth people to travel to. (Those would be RAMS and SUVEN in the puzzle here.)

Are you familiar enough with the names of the planets to be able to unscramble them?

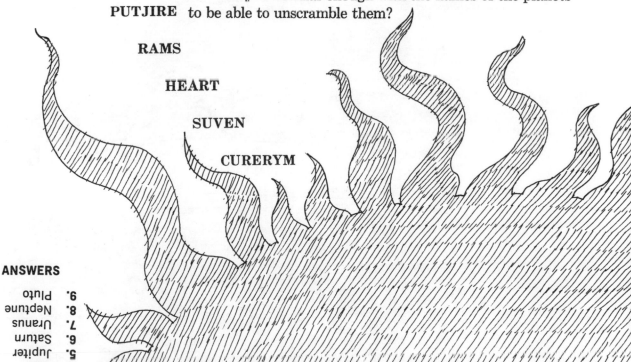

ANSWERS

1. Mercury
2. Venus
3. Earth
4. Mars
5. Jupiter
6. Saturn
7. Uranus
8. Neptune
9. Pluto

A BATUNTROZ *WHAT?*

In 1904, a cartoonist depicted what he thought a certain object would look like in the future. From the cartoon, it's hard to tell what he had in mind. But if you take the letters on the object and write down every other letter, you will find out what this drawing represents. After you do, you might want to make a sketch of your own of what you think this object will look like in the future.

ANSWER:

Automobile

MEASURING THE FUTURE

When it comes to measuring, the future is happening right now, for we are already beginning to use the metric system in our daily lives.

The old system of weights and measures is pretty much unchanged from the time when we were colonies of England. Today, the only major countries still using that system are the United States and the British Commonwealth nations.

Are You Ready to Measure the Future?

Here's a good way to find out.

10 KILOGRAMS   22 POUNDS

Which is greater . . .

1. A meter or a yard?

2. A centimeter or an inch?

3. A kilometer or a mile?

4. A liter (liquid measure) or a quart?

5. A kilogram or a pound?

6. A liter (dry measure) or a quart?

7. A hectare or an acre?

Now ask your parents to answer those questions. Chances are you will do as well or better than they do.

ANSWERS

1. A meter (about 39⅓ inches, compared with 36 inches)
2. An inch (2.5 centimeters)
3. A mile (1.6 kilometers)
4. A liter (1.06 quarts)
5. A kilogram (2.2 pounds)
6. A quart (1.101 liters)
7. A hectare (2.5 acres)

HOW WILL HISTORIANS IN THE YEAR 2025 LEARN ABOUT TODAY?

To learn about our lives today, future historians will certainly use—

A. Newspapers

B. Tapes of TV programs

C. Conversations with people like you who lived through the times

D. Photographs

E. Paintings

F. The clothing, furniture, tools, and many other objects used in daily living

G. Magazines and books.

Now, if you were writing a history of the thirteen English colonies, which of those items could you use?

1. A, B, E, and G

2. A, C, E, and F

3. A, E, F, and G

4. A, D, F, and G

ANSWER

Number 3. There was no TV and no photography, and nobody is still living from the colonial period. A historian could use newspapers, paintings, clothing, and other objects, and magazines and books of the times.

MAKE YOUR OWN TIME CAPSULE

Here is a really nice way to spend a rainy day or a day when you are sick and cannot go to school. Make your own time capsule.

A time capsule contains information about the present that is preserved so that people in the future will be able to know about how we lived. For example, at the World's Fair held in New York in 1938, a time capsule was buried which contained many items, including—

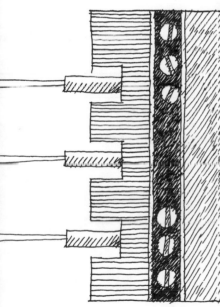

Books and pictures of how we live
Descriptions of office and business machines
Histories of sports, theaters, motion pictures
Advertisements
The Holy Bible
A copy of our Constitution
A chronological history of the world
A history of the United States
A dictionary
The Lord's Prayer in 300 languages
Farm produce
Samples of the clothes in style at the time
Cosmetics
Copies of newspapers and magazines
Stories of our scientific achievements
Descriptions of our architecture.

You might use a shoe box for your time capsule and put it away in a closet or attic for safekeeping. You might plan to open it anytime in the future, perhaps in five or ten years. What you put in your time capsule is up to you, but here are some suggestions:

A photograph of yourself and members of your family
A family tree that you have made up (See page 95.)
The names of your friends, classmates, and teachers
Samples of your schoolwork, including poems and stories that you have written
A list of your favorite books, movies, TV shows, songs, and teams.

NOW IT'S YOUR TURN . . .

To Write Your Own History

History is not only about famous people and events. You too are a part of history, and so is your family. It's fun to learn about your family, and one way to do it is to make a family tree, like the one in the cartoon.

How far back in your family's history can you go? To your grandparents? To your great-grandparents? Beyond that?

Were your parents born in the same part of the country where you were born? Perhaps they were born in a different part of the world, or maybe their parents were.

Talk to some of the older members of the family. They can probably tell you a lot of surprising things about what life was like when they were children. And while we're on the subject, what things about your childhood do you think you will be telling your own children?

Whatever they are, that is your very own history. And that makes it important.

Remember Grant,
Remember Lee,
The heck with them,
Remember me.